Jul 2018

JACK THE RIPPER

This series features unsolved mysteries, urban legends, and other curious stories. Each creepy, shocking, or befuddling book focuses on what people believe and hear. True or not? That's for you to decide!

45th Parallel Press

Published in the United States of America by Cherry Lake Publishing
Ann Arbor, Michigan
www.cherrylakepublishing.com

Author: Virginia Loh-Hagan
Reading Adviser: Marla Conn MS, Ed., Literacy specialist, Read-Ability, Inc.
Book Designer: Felicia Macheske

Photo Credits: © Dm_Cherry/Shutterstock.com, cover; © Valery Sidelnykov/Shutterstock.com, 5; © rock-the-stock/
Shutterstock.com, 7; © Arman Zhenikeyev/Shutterstock.com, 8, 11; © Dubova/Shutterstock.com, 13; © David
Burrows/Shutterstock.com, 15; © XiXinXing/Shutterstock.com, 16; © Christian Delbert/Shutterstock.com, 18;
© nw10photography/Shutterstock.com, 21; © KathySG/Shutterstock.com, 22; © Rawpixel.com/Shutterstock.com, 24;
© Nomad_Soul/Shutterstock.com, 27; © carlos castilla/Shutterstock.com, 29

Graphic Elements Throughout: © iofoto/Shutterstock.com; © COLCU/Shutterstock.com; © spacedrone808/
Shutterstock.com; © rf.vector.stock/Shutterstock.com; © donatas1205/Shutterstock.com; © cluckva/
Shutterstock.com; © Eky Studio/Shutterstock.com

45th Parallel Press is an imprint of Cherry Lake Publishing.

Library of Congress Cataloging-in-Publication Data

Names: Loh-Hagan, Virginia, author.
Title: Jack the Ripper / by Dr. Virginia Loh-Hagan.
Description: Loh-Hagan, Virginia : Cherry Lake Publishing, [2018] | Series:
 Urban legends : don't read alone! | Audience: Grade 4 to 6. | Includes
 bibliographical references and index.
Identifiers: LCCN 2017033729| ISBN 9781534107656 (hardcover) | ISBN
 9781534109636 (pdf) | ISBN 9781534108646 (pbk.) | ISBN 9781534120624
 (hosted ebook)
Subjects: LCSH: Jack, the Ripper—Juvenile literature. | Serial
 murders—England—London—History—19th century—Juvenile literature. |
 Serial murder investigation—England—London—History—19th
 century—Juvenile literature. | Whitechapel (London,
 England)—History—Juvenile literature.
Classification: LCC HV6535.G6 L63725 2018 | DDC 364.152/32092—dc23
LC record available at https://lccn.loc.gov/2017033729

Cherry Lake Publishing would like to acknowledge the work of The Partnership for 21st Century Skills.
Please visit *www.p21.org* for more information.

Printed in the United States of America
Corporate Graphics

TABLE OF CONTENTS

Chapter One

FIVE UNFORTUNATE FEMALES

Who are the five women murdered by Jack the Ripper? How were they similar? How were they different?

Jack the Ripper was a **serial** killer. Serial means more than one. Jack killed women. He killed them in similar ways. He's known for killing 5 women. He may have killed more women. He killed them in Whitechapel. Whitechapel is a town in England.

Mary Ann Nichols was the first **victim**. Victims are people who suffer from crimes. Nichols was killed on August 31, 1888. Her body was found. Five teeth were missing. Her tongue was cut out. Her throat was cut open. Her face had bruises. Her stomach was ripped out. She had other small cuts. The cuts were down to her bone.

Nichols was around 30 years old when she was killed.

CONSIDER THE EVIDENCE

Whitechapel is in the East End of London. It's close to the ship docks. It's outside the city walls. It has a famous history. It was a popular place for immigrants. It was a popular place for the working class. There was overcrowding. Too many people lived there. Many people were poor. They were homeless. They lived in the street. Some people had jobs. But the jobs were bad. Working conditions were poor. All this made people desperate. Desperate means doing anything to survive. There was a lot of crime. There was a lot of violence. There was a lot of alcohol abuse. There was a lot of sickness.

Annie Chapman was the second victim. Her body was found on September 8, 1888. She had a swollen face. She had a swollen mouth. Her throat was cut. Her stomach was ripped out. Her **organs** were ripped out. Organs are parts from inside the body. Some people thought Jack might be a doctor.

Elizabeth Stride was the third victim. She was found on September 30, 1888. Her killing was different. She didn't have as many cuts. Her cuts seemed less **precise**. Precise means skilled or correct. Her body was found near a busy restaurant. Some people think Jack was spotted and ran. He didn't get to finish the job.

All of the victims, besides Nichols, were in their mid-40s.

There was a note written on Eddowes door from the killer.

Catherine Eddowes was the fourth victim. She was also found on September 30, 1888. She had deep cuts. Cuts were on her face, throat, and stomach. Her organs were ripped out. A piece of her apron was found. There was blood on it. Jack may have wiped his knife on it.

Mary Jane Kelly was the fifth victim. She was found on November 9, 1888. Her face was cut up. Her body parts were cut off. Her organs were ripped out. Her heart was missing. Her killing was the most violent. Jack had more time. He killed her in her room. The others were killed in the street.

Chapter Two

MYSTERY KILLER

How were the killings similar? How did Jack get away? What is Jack the Ripper's profile?

These five women were killed at night. They were killed around the beginning and end of the month. They were killed on weekends. They had similar cuts. Each killing got more violent. The killer did more damage each time. Experts link these killings to one man. They call him Jack the Ripper. No one knew who he was. Even today, people don't know who he is.

He was never caught. There are many ideas about how got away. Jack may have blended into the crowd. He may have used the tunnels under the city.

Jack the Ripper is also known as the "Whitechapel Murderer" and the "Leather Apron."

SPOTLIGHT
BIOGRAPHY

Cressida Rose Dick was born in 1960. She's the commissioner of the Metropolitan Police in London, England. She's in charge of Scotland Yard. She's the top police officer. She's the first woman to do this. She started on April 10, 2017. Dick became a cop in 1983. She kept getting promoted. She got her master's degree in criminology. This is the study of crimes. Dick got the highest grade in her class. She supports women in top cop positions. She said this would "send a strong message" that Scotland Yard was "modern and representative." She's known for being honest. She's known for making good decisions.

Experts studied the killings. They made guesses about Jack. They thought about how he killed. They thought about when he killed. They used what they knew. They created a **profile**. Profiles are quick descriptions of people.

Jack may have had a normal job during the week. He may have been between 25 and 30 years old. He may have lived in Whitechapel. He may have been medium height. He may have had a thick body. He may have had a mustache. He seemed to know how to use a knife. He seemed to understand how bodies worked. He may have been single. He may have had **insomnia**. Insomnia means not being able to sleep.

Some experts thought Jack had issues with his mother.

Chapter Three

MANHUNT!

Who searched for Jack the Ripper? Who was George Hutchinson?

Scotland Yard is the headquarters for London cops. It's famous. It's known for having the best **detectives**. Detectives are cops who solve crimes. They looked for Jack the Ripper. Detectives went to each house in Whitechapel. They asked questions. They talked to over 2,000 people. They investigated over 300 people. They took evidence. They questioned **suspects**. They found 80 suspects. Suspects are people accused of committing crimes.

Butchers and doctors were the number one suspects. More than 75 butchers were interviewed. They had **alibis**. Alibis are claims suspects make that show they're not guilty. They are meant to prove the suspect was not at the scene of the crime.

Scotland Yard is one of the world's oldest police forces.

Today, citizens form neighborhood watch groups.

People in Whitechapel got scared. They weren't happy with the cops. They were upset that the cops hadn't found the killer yet. They didn't want a killer on the loose. They formed a group. They formed the Whitechapel **Vigilance** Committee. Vigilance means keeping a careful watch. This group walked the streets. They looked for people doing odd things. They hired private detectives. They wanted information about the killer. They asked the government to offer **rewards**. Rewards are money. Money would be given to people who shared information.

REAL-WORLD
CONNECTION

Gaynor Issitt lives in England. She lives in a haunted house. She's lived there for 36 years. The ghost who haunts the house attacks her. She said the ghost was there before she moved in. The ghost drags Issitt out of bed. It pulls her ankles. It punches her. It hits her on the head. It burns Bibles. Issitt said, "I'll never move out. I love my home. All my kids were brought up here. And I won't be bullied out by a ghost … I've just learned to live with it." Issitt has called priests. She's called ghost experts. She said these people run away screaming. Mark Vernon is a ghost hunter. He visited Issitt's house. He said the ghost could be Jack the Ripper.

Multiple witnesses are helpful when solving a crime.

There were several **witnesses**. Witnesses are people who see something related to a crime. People reported seeing some of the victims with a man.

George Hutchinson was a witness. He lived in Whitechapel. He saw Kelly on the night she was killed. He saw a man with her. He gave a lot of details. He described the man's hair. He described the man's boots. Then Hutchinson disappeared. Some people think he was Jack the Ripper. They think he pretended to see another man. They think he made up details. They think he did this to confuse the cops.

Chapter Four

USUAL AND UNUSUAL SUSPECTS

Who are some famous people accused of being Jack the Ripper? Who is Jill the Ripper? What are some other ideas about Jack the Ripper?

Some people think Jack the Ripper was Prince Albert Victor. The prince is Queen Victoria's grandson. He had a sickness. People thought he lost his mind. They thought he killed women during this time. Officials said the prince was nowhere near the area.

Some people accused Walter Sickert. Sickert was a famous painter. He painted nude women. He was probably in France during the killings.

Some accused Lewis Carroll. Carroll was a famous author. He wrote *Alice in Wonderland*. Some accused Randolph Churchill. Churchill was Sir Winston Churchill's father. Churchill looked like Hutchinson's description.

There are more than 100 named suspects.

Most people assume the killer was a male. But some disagree. They think Jack the Ripper was a female. They believe in "Jill the Ripper." Everyone was looking for a male. This means a female killer would have more chances to go unnoticed.

People accused Mary Pearcey. Pearcey was an English woman. She killed a woman and her baby. She did it with a knife. She dumped their bodies in the street. This happened in 1890. The killings were similar to the Whitechapel killings.

The killer could have dressed in the victim's clothes to confuse people.

INVESTIGATION TIPS

- Talk to police officers. Ask them how they solve crimes. Get some tips.

- Write everything down. Take good notes. Details matter.

- Follow every lead. Leads are ideas. Don't get stuck on one idea. Explore different ideas.

- Search the area. Every contact leaves a trace. Consider everything as evidence. Look for connections.

- Talk to witnesses right away. People forget things over time. They may add details. They may decide not to talk. The best reports are done soon after the incident.

- Ask a lot of questions. Try to find a motive. Motives are reasons for doing things.

Some people who study history think Jack the Ripper never existed.

Some people thought the killer was a **midwife**. Midwives are women. They're like doctors for women. They deliver babies. They could work at night. They could have blood on their clothes. They know about the human body. Some called the killer "The Mad Midwife."

Some people believe in other ideas. Some think the cops killed the women. They think cops made up Jack the Ripper. They think cops did this to cover up their crimes.

Some think the Russian secret police killed the women. They think the Russians wanted to make the London cops look bad.

Chapter Five

THREE STRANGE LETTERS

How did Jack the Ripper get his name? What are the three most important letters? Are the letters real or fake?

The cops got hundreds of letters. There were three important letters.

The first letter was dated September 27, 1888. It's called the "Dear Boss" letter. The letter was signed from "Jack the Ripper." This was the first time the name was used. That's how the killer got his name.

The second letter was a postcard. It was dated

October 1, 1888. It's called the "Saucy Jacky" letter. It's signed from "Jack the Ripper." It shared details about the killing of Stride and Eddowes. It called the killings the "double event."

Most of the letters were useless.

EXPLAINED BY SCIENCE

Today, many murder cases are solved by DNA testing. DNA lives in cells. It's in our bodies, It tells our bodies how to live. It's our bodies' code. About 99.9 percent of every person's DNA is the same. It's that 0.1 percent that makes us all special. It's how people can be identified. People touch things. This leaves DNA. People's blood has DNA. Their spit has DNA. Their skin has DNA. Criminals may leave DNA behind. Police and scientists search crime scenes. They may find DNA. They study the DNA. The use special machines. They check for links between the suspects and DNA. DNA testing narrows down the suspects. It's 95 percent correct.

The third letter was the "From Hell" letter. It was dated on October 16, 1888. It was sent to George Lusk. Lusk was the leader of the Whitechapel Vigilance Committee. The letter came with a small box. The box had half a kidney in it. Eddowes's kidney was removed. Some thought it was a match.

The letters were written in the same way. The handwriting was the same. But some people didn't believe the letters. They thought the letters were fake. They thought people were playing jokes. They thought newspapers made up the letters to make news.

Real or not? It doesn't matter. Jack the Ripper lives in people's imaginations.

There wasn't enough proof to identify the killer.

DID YOU KNOW?

- Ripperology is the study of Jack the Ripper. Ripperologists are the people who study Jack the Ripper.

- Over 4,000 books have been written about Jack the Ripper.

- Queen Victoria thought Jack the Ripper was a butcher or a cattle drover. Butchers cut and sell meat. Cattle drovers move cattle over long distances.

- Cops thought about using dogs to find Jack the Ripper. But they decided not to. There were too many smells in Whitechapel. Cops worried that criminals would poison the dogs.

- Robert James Lees was a psychic. Psychics see the future. Lees went to Scotland Yard. He offered to find Jack the Ripper. Cops turned him away. They called him a "fool."

- Scotland Yard stands on the site of a medieval palace. It belonged to Scottish royalty. The Scots lived there when they came to London. That's how Scotland Yard got its name.

- John Douglas works for the FBI. He's an expert on serial killers. He studied Jack the Ripper. He created a profile of the killer.

- Scotland Yard won a legal battle in May 2011. It doesn't want to share the Jack the Ripper files. It wants to protect witnesses and their families.

CONSIDER THIS!

Take a Position: Who is Jack the Ripper? Learn more about the suspects. Which one do you think is most likely to be Jack the Ripper? Explain your thinking. Argue your point with reasons and evidence.

Say What? Reread the page about Jill the Ripper. It's from chapter 4. Explain why some people think Jack the Ripper is a female. What do you think about this idea?

Think About It! Jack the Ripper was a murderer. Murder is a crime. He broke laws. He hurt people. If he were caught, how would you punish him? Punishments should fit the crime.

LEARN MORE

- Burgan, Michael. *Jack the Ripper*. New York: Aladdin, 2017.
- Debois, Francois, and Jean-Charles Poupard (illus.). *Jack the Ripper*. Milwaukie, OR: Dark Horse Books, 2015.

GLOSSARY

alibis (AL-uh-byez) claims that a suspect was somewhere else when a crime was committed

detectives (dih-TEK-tivz) people who solve crimes and mysteries

insomnia (in-SAHM-nee-uh) not being able to sleep

midwife (MID-wife) a female medical professional who helps women deliver babies and takes care of women's health issues

organs (OR-guhnz) body parts that are inside the body like kidney, heart, and lungs

precise (prih-SISE) accurate, correct, skilled

profile (PROH-file) quick description of someone

rewards (rih-WARDZ) money or prizes given for doing something

serial (SEER-ee-uhl) part of a series, more than one

suspects (SUH-spekts) people who are accused of committing a crime

victim (VIK-tuhm) a person who suffers from a crime

vigilance (VIJ-uh-luhns) keeping a careful watch

witnesses (WIT-nis-iz) people who see something

INDEX

ABOUT THE AUTHOR

Dr. Virginia Loh-Hagan is an author, university professor, former classroom teacher, and curriculum designer. She loves British history, culture, and literature. She lives in San Diego with her very tall husband and very naughty dogs. To learn more about her, visit www.virginialoh.com.